KEY

- Species marked with
- Species marked with
- Species marked with these icons **V** or **B** are either an aesthetic garden visitor or a beneficial predator of pest species.
- Species marked with this icon **D** spread plant disease.

GARDEN BUGS OF THE NORTHWEST

In everyday language, we commonly refer to insects, spiders, and other creepy-crawly organisms, such as centipedes, as bugs. They, or signs of their presence, are routinely encountered in gardens and yards. Within this diverse mix are a wide variety of "bad" bugs, regularly referred to as pests, and "good" bugs, which are often considered beneficial. Most garden pest species cause damage by directly feeding on plants, transmitting disease to plants in the process, or by indirectly damaging or disturbing plants by their activities. The resulting damage can be simply aesthetic or can lead to poor plant performance, deformed growth, reduced yield, or even death. Other pests can cause damage to structures or present a nuisance by their presence.

Beneficial species are a gardener's best friends. They provide natural pest control by feeding on or parasitizing undesirable garden and landscape bugs, helping to keep their populations in check. Others deliver key services such as decomposition, nutrient recycling, or pollination. Many are also entertaining or attractive and add to the overall enjoyment of the garden.

Controlling Pests

It's temping to want to reach for a container of pesticide at the first sign of a pest problem. This strategy, however, can often be counterproductive. Many commonly available pesticides can be harmful to humans, other wildlife, and the environment, especially if overused or applied inappropriately. Beneficial insects, such as monarchs and bees, are particularly susceptible. Harming these "good" bugs depletes your garden's natural pest control measures.

A better and more sustainable approach is to use integrated pest management, referred to as IPM. IPM focuses on long-term prevention, not just short-term control. Monitoring is the first step. This is best done by regularly getting out into your garden or landscape and looking around. Do you see any obvious signs of pest presence or plant problems? If you do, take a closer look and try to identify the culprit. Use this guide as an aid. You can then take a sample to a local extension agent or nursery professional for confirmation. Next, it's important to assess the scope of the problem. Is it limited to a particular branch or plant, or is it impacting a larger area or number of plants? No matter what, regular monitoring is always a great strategy, as it helps you identify pest issues before they become problems. Remember, most large pest outbreaks start out small.

Now that you have identified the pest and level of infestation, you can develop a plan to control it or decide that control is not required at this particular time. IPM employs a management approach that typically involves a combination of mechanical, biological, and chemical controls to specifically target the pest of concern.

Removing aphids by hand or with a hard spray of water from a hose is a mechanical control option

Mechanical control can include physically removing pests from plants, using traps or barriers, or otherwise making a less suitable or desirable environment for the pest.

Biological control uses known natural enemies against the pest. This can be a predator, parasitoid, or even a pathogen. A classic example is using ladybugs to help control aphids.

Ladybugs are a popular biological control option.

Chemical control, especially broad-spectrum insecticides, should be a last resort.

Chemical control makes use of pesticides. Pesticides should only be used when necessary. Less-toxic alternatives such as horticultural oils or insecticidal soaps are often used first, and treatments are always applied only to the infected plant to minimize nontarget impacts. Remember, when using chemicals, always carefully follow the label directions for application rates and safety precautions.

Healthy & Diverse Landscapes

Healthy plants are more resistant to attack from pests and disease. Therefore, regular garden care and maintenance, along with a little TLC, is a great way to help prevent problems. Healthy plants also look and perform better, produce more flowers, and offer higher quality resources for pollinators.

Healthy plants, like this bee balm, will welcome beneficial insects and resist pests more effectively.

Landscapes with higher levels of plant diversity, particularly flowering plants, tend to attract and maintain a higher abundance and wider range of beneficial insects. Collectively, such basic methods are easy to implement and offer a strong first line of defense.

A variety of blooming plants, especially native species, invites beneficial pollinators to your yard.

Good Plants for Beneficials

Beyond preying on pest species, many beneficial insects also feed on pollen and nectar. They are therefore attracted to landscapes with an ample supply of floral resources. While there is no shortage of wonderful blooming plants to choose from, there are some basic tried-and-true (and readily available) choices. These include many common bedding plants, wildflowers, and herbs.

Common herbs, such as this dill, attract many pollinators.

If allowed to flower, dill, fennel, borage, rosemary, thyme, mint, and basil are magnets for beneficial species.

Many daisy-like flowers (Asteraceae) such as zinnias, cosmos, Indian blanket, purple coneflower, coreopsis, goldenrod, and sunflowers are equally attractive.

Sunflowers and other profusely flowering plants make your yard an insect magnet.

Dutch White Clover, while non-native, is a great option to make a bare spot on a lawn or a garden more attractive to wildlife.

Lastly, clovers, partridge pea, dotted horsemint, buckwheat, and sweet alyssum are all fantastic. Whether planted alongside vegetables in the home garden, included more broadly in the larger landscape, or simply placed in a container or window box, they will not fail to provide color and attraction.

Silver-spotted Skipper 🦋 Ⓥ
(Epargyreus clarus)

wingspan up to 2.4 inches; stout body; wings brown with a prominent white patch on the hindwing below; larvae feed on various pea family plants, including *Wisteria* spp. and honey locust (*Gleditsia triacanthos*); larvae make leaf shelters

Common Checkered Skipper 🦋 Ⓥ
(Pyrgus communis)

wingspan up to 1.5 inches; wings black with scattered white spots; hindwing below white with tan bands; often feeds and perches with wings open; larvae feed on various mallow family plants

Anise Swallowtail 🦋 Ⓥ
(Papilio zelicaon)

wingspan up to 3.8 inches; wings black with a broad central yellow band, marginal yellow spots and a black-centered hindwing eyespot; hindwing with single tail; larvae feed on members of the carrot family

Anise Swallowtail Larva 🦋 Ⓥ Ⓟ
(Papilio zelicaon)

up to 2 inches in length; green body with black bands that contain yellow-orange spots

Western Tiger Swallowtail 🦋 Ⓥ
(Papilio rutulus)

wingspan up to 4 inches; wings yellow with bold black stripes, a wide black margin, and a single long tail; avid flower visitor

Pale Swallowtail 🦋 Ⓥ
(Papilio eurymedon)

wingspan up to 3.5 inches; wings white with bold black stripes and a single hindwing tail

Two-tailed Swallowtail
(Papilio multicaudata)

wingspan up to 6 inches; wings yellow with bold black stripes, black margins, and two hindwing tails; avid flower visitor

Cabbage White
(Pieris rapae)

wingspan up to 2 inches; wings white with black forewing tops and black spots; female with 2 spots, male with one spot; non-native; accidentally introduced from Europe; agricultural and garden pest

Cabbage White Larva
(Pieris rapae)

up to 1.1 inches long; green to bluish green body with short hairs and a fine yellow side stripe; larvae are considered pests of various cruciferous vegetables including cabbage, broccoli, cauliflower, and kale

Orange Sulphur
(Colias eurytheme)

wingspan up to 2.5 inches; wings orange with black borders in male; yellow-orange in females; forewing with black cell spot; some females white; hindwing below yellow with central pink-rimmed silver spot; larvae feed on clovers and alfalfa

Woodland Skipper
(Ochlodes sylvanoides)

wingspan up to 1.25 inches; wings above orange with jagged brown borders; hindwing below tawny brown with a pale spot band; larvae feed on grasses

Purplish Copper 🦋 Ⓥ
(Lycaena helloides)

wingspan up to 1.25 inches; wings above brown with distinct purple sheen in males; females with more orange scaling; hindwing below gray-brown with narrow wavy orange line along the outer margin

Gray Hairstreak 🦋 Ⓥ
(Strymon melinus)

wingspan up to 1.4 inches; wings above dark gray with orange-capped black spot on hindwing; hindwing below light gray with white-outlined black line and orange-capped black spots near single hair-like tail; avid flower visitor

Monarch 🦋 Ⓥ
(Danaus plexippus)

wingspan up to 5 inches; wings orange with black veins and borders; avid flower visitor; migratory; larvae feed on milkweeds

Monarch Larva Ⓥ
(Danaus plexippus)

up to 2 inches long; banded with yellow, white, and black; has two black filaments on each end; feeds on milkweeds; populations declining

Great Spangled Fritillary 🦋 Ⓥ
(Speyeria cybele)

wingspan up to 3.5 inches; wings tawny orange with black spots and bands in male; wings dark brown with broad pale borders in female; hindwing below tawny orange to dark brown with silvery spots and a broad pale band along the outer margin

Mylitta Crescent 🔘 Ⓥ
(Phyciodes mylitta)

wingspan up to 1.4 inches; wings above tawny orange with dark borders, spots, and lines; hindwing below tan to light tawny orange with darker bands and spots and a light crescent-shaped spot along the outer margin

Red Admiral 🔘 Ⓥ
(Vanessa atalanta)

wingspan up to 3 inches; wings above black with reddish-orange bands; forewing with white apical spots; larvae feed on false nettle, pellitory, and nettles; particularly common in spring

Mourning Cloak Ⓥ
(Nymphalis antiopa)

wingspan up to 3.5 inches; wings above brownish-black with jagged margins, a broad yellow border and blue spots; wings below black with gray striations resembling bark; adults do not visit flowers but feed on tree sap and fermenting fruit

Painted Lady 🔘 Ⓥ
(Vanessa cardui)

wingspan up to 2.5 inches; wings orange with black spots, forewing with black tip containing white spots; hindwing below mottled brown, cream, and black with a row of small eyespots; larvae feed on thistles

West Coast Lady 🔘 Ⓥ
(Vanessa annabella)

wingspan up to 2.2 inches; wings orange with black markings; forewing with white spots near a squared-off tip; hindwing with a row of blue-centered eyespots; larvae feed on mallow family plants

Common Ringlet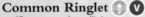
(Coenonympha tullia)

wingspan up to 1.5 inches; variable;
wings below orange-brown to gray,
darker toward the base, with white
central band

Eastern Tailed-blue
(Cupido comyntas)

wingspan up to 1 inch; wings bright
blue in males, brown in females; wings
below light gray with black spots; hindwing with orange-capped black spot
near a single short tail

Echo Azure
(Celastrina echo)

wingspan up to 1.25 inches; wings
above unmarked pale blue in males;
forewing blue with dark borders in
females; wings below whitish-gray
with small dark spots and lines

California Tortoiseshell
(Nymphalis californica)

wingspan up to 2.7 inches; wings tawny
orange with dark spots and an irregular
dark border; forewing tip squared off;
wings below mottled brown and barklike; adults overwinter

Lorquin's Admiral
(Limenitis lorquini)

wingspan up to 2.5 inches; wings above
black with broad white central bands,
white forewing cell spot, and orange
forewing tips; wings bellow reddish-
brown with white markings as above

Milbert's Tortoiseshell
(Aglais milberti)

wingspan to 2.25 inches; wings above
black with broad orange irregular orange
border and orange forewing cell spots;
hindwing with small blue spots along
the margin; forewing tip squared off;
wings below dark brownish-black with
broad lighter brown band

Ceanothus Silkmoth Ⓥ
(Hyalophora euryalus)

wingspan up to 5 inches; wings above reddish-brown with narrow white band, central crescent-shaped white spots, and pale borders; forewing tip with a single dark eyespot; hairy red-and-white body; ferny antennae

Five-spotted Hawkmoth ⬤ Ⓥ
(Manduca quinquemaculata)

wingspan up to 5.5 inches; wings elongated; forewing gray with barklike patterns, hindwing light gray with darker lines; abdomen with yellow side spots; feeds like a hummingbird; larvae feed on tomatoes, peppers, and eggplants

Five-spotted Hawkmoth Larva Ⓟ
(Manduca quinquemaculata)

up to 3 inches; green with white diagonal stripes and a curved horn off the rear; pupates underground

White-lined Sphinx ⬤ Ⓥ
(Hyles lineata)

wingspan up to 3.8 inches; wings and body elongated; forewing brown with cream veins and a central cream stripe; hindwing brown with central pink band; feeds like a hummingbird at flowers; larvae feed on a wide range of plants in multiple families

White-lined Sphinx Larva Ⓥ Ⓟ
(Hyles lineata)

up to 3.5 inches long; highly variable in color; green with black and yellow markings and a curved horn off the rear; pupates underground

Polyphemus Moth Ⓥ
(Antheraea polyphemus)

wingspan up to 5.8 inches; wings tan to warm brown; hindwing with large eyespot; males with large ferny antennae; adults regularly come to lights at night

Polyphemus Moth Larva Ⓥ
(Antheraea polyphemus)

up to 3 inches long; bright green body with thin yellow vertical stripes and a brown head; larvae feed on various trees and shrubs

Wild Cherry Sphinx Ⓔ Ⓥ
(Sphinx drupiferarum)

wingspan up to 4.3 inches; elongated wings; wings above dark gray with light gray borders and lines; wings below light gray

Western Poplar Sphinx Ⓥ
(Pachysphinx occidentalis)

wingspan up to 5.8 inches; elongated wings; forewing above variable from mottled light brown to mottled darker olive-brown; hindwing with rosy patch and dark eyespot; adults do not feed; adults come to artificial lights at night

Cinnabar Moth Ⓥ
(Tyria jacobaeae)

wingspan up to 0.75 inches; forewing black with red band along leading margin and red spots along outer margin; hindwing unmarked red with narrow black border; adults day flying; introduced as biological control for invasive tansy ragwort

Red–Shouldered Ctenucha Ⓥ
(Ctenucha rubroscapus)

wingspan up to 1.9 inches; wings dull black; forewing with narrow white band at tip; iridescent blue body; thorax with red shoulders; head red; adults day flying and visit flowers

Isabella Tiger Moth Ⓥ
(Pyrrharctia isabella)

wingspan up to 2.5 inches; forewing yellow-brown with pointed tip and faint darker markings; hindwing lighter yellow in males, pinkish-orange in females; adults attracted to lights at night

Banded Woollybear **V**
(Pyrrharctia isabella)

up to 2.25 inches long; densely fuzzy; banded with black at both ends and reddish-brown in the middle; abdomen yellow-orange with black spots

Spotted Tussock Moth **V**
(Lophocampa maculata)

up to 1.7 inches; forewing above yellow with darker brown bands; hindwing light yellow to cream; adults come to artificial lights at night

Spotted Tussock Moth Larva **V**
(Lophocampa maculata)

up to 1.1 inches long; hairy; black on both ends with yellow or orange in the middle; ends bear elongated white hair tufts; feed on various trees

Garden Tiger Moth **V**
(Arctia caja)

wingspan up to 2.5 inches; forewing above dark brown with irregular interconnecting white bands; hindwing orange with round black-rimmed dark blue spots; adults attracted to artificial lights at night

Western Tent Caterpillar **P**
(Malacosoma californicum)

up to 2 inches long; color somewhat variable; blue-gray and orange marked with black; covered in long pale hairs that are orange toward the base; feeds together in large silken webs; spring pest of various landscape trees; feeds on numerous forest trees and shrubs including some fruit trees; foliage pest that causes primarily aesthetic damage in home landscapes

Cabbage Looper **P**
(Trichoplusia ni)

up to 1.5 inches long; light green with thin light stripe on the side; moves like an inchworm; pest of various vegetables and flowers; readily feeds on cabbage, kale, broccoli, cauliflower, and collards

Inchworm **V P**
(Family Geometridae)

length variable; but generally 0.5–1 inch long; color variable from green to brown; larvae of geometer moths; have only two pairs of prolegs on the abdomen; move by holding on with front legs and moving rear forward causing the central part of the body to raise up

Morning-glory Plume Moth **V P**
(Emmelina monodactyla)

wingspan up to 1 inch; color variable from whitish to brown; long narrow body and long legs; wings rolled at rest to form narrow "T" shape with body; adults attracted to artificial lights at night; larvae feed on plants in the morning glory family

Columbian Emerald Moth **V P**
(Nemoria darwiniata)

wingspan up to 1.2 inches; wings bright green with thin pale line through the center; abdomen with pink and white spots; adults attacted to artificial lights at night

Winter Moth **P**
(Operophtera brumata)

wingspan to 1 inch; forewings rounded in males; forewings mottled light brown to gray brown; hindwings paler; females are flightless with wings reduced to nubs; invasive; larvae feed on various trees and shrubs; adults found in winter

European Ground Beetle **B**
(Carabus nemoralis)

up to 1 inch long; flattened, oval shiny bronze-black body; head with notice-able mandibles; introduced from Europe; adults and larvae are predaceous

Ten-lined June Beetle **P**
(Polyphylla decemlineata)

up to 1.25 inches long; brown oval body marked with vertical white stripes and noticeably clubbed antennae; larvae live in the soil and feed on plant roots; causes injury to fruit trees, vege-tables, and landscape plants

Bee-mimic Beetle ⊕ **V**
(Trichiotinus assimilis)

up to 0.50 inch long; stout brown-black body; wing cases marked with gold and two pale stripes; noticeably hairy abdomen

Western Eyed Click Beetle **V**
(Alaus melanops)

up to 1.4 inches long; narrow, oval slate gray-black body mottled with white; thorax with two large white-rimmed black eyespots; long antennae; larvae feed on dead wood; adults attracted to artificial lights at night

Ornate Checkered Beetle **V**
(Trichodes ornatus)

up to 0.5 inch; narrow oval body; thorax copper colored; wing coverings iridescent blue-black with irregular yellow bands; adults visit flowers and feed on pollen

Colorado Potato Beetle **P**
(Leptinotarsa decemlineata)

up to 0.4 inch long; oval, cream-to-tan body with black stripes and a slightly orange thorax (pronotum) marked with black; bulbous larvae are reddish marked with black spots; pest of various potato, eggplant, and tomato

Spotted Cucumber Beetle P D
(Diabrotica undecimpunctata)

up to 0.35 inch long; black head; yellow wing coverings with black spots; adults and larvae feed on squash, cucumbers, pumpkins, and melons

Spotted Asparagus Beetle P
(Crioceris duodecimpunctata)

up to 0.25 inch long; reddish-orange wing coverings with 12 black spots; adults and larvae feed on asparagus

Common Asparagus Beetle P
(Crioceris asparagi)

up to 0.3 inch long; head black, thorax orange; wing coverings dark bluish-green with cream spots and orange along the margin; adults and larvae feed on asparagus

Asian Lady Beetle P B
(Harmonia axyridis)

up to 0.35 inch; oval body; pattern highly variable from unmarked orange to red with black spots; invasive; adults invade homes and other structures to overwinter; displacing native lady beetles; adults and larvae feed on other insects, including many pest species

Two-spotted Lady Beetle B
(Adalia bipunctata)

up to 0.2 inch long; round body; wing covering shiny red with two black spots; dark form is black with generally 4 red spots; adults and larvae predaceous

Seven-spotted Lady Beetle B
(Coccinella septempunctata)

up to 0.3 inch long; round-to-oval body; thorax black with two white spots; wing coverings reddish-orange with 7 black spots; adults and larvae feed on aphids and other soft-bodied plant pests

BEETLES (side tab)

Western Polished Lady Beetle
(Cycloneda polita)

up to 0.25 inch long; round body; wing coverings shiny unmaked red to orange-red; thorax black with white lines that form a "C" on both sides

Lady Beetle Larva ⑧
(Family Coccinellidae)

up to 0.25 inch long; elongated black body with orange spots; resembles a tiny alligator; highly beneficial predator of insect eggs and soft-bodied pests, including mites, aphids, thrips, and mealybugs

Three-banded Lady Beetle ⑧
(Coccinella trifasciata)

up to 0.2 inch long; round body; variable pattern; wing covering shiny red with three orange-bordered black spot bands; adults and larvae predaceous

White-spotted Sawyer Beetle ℗
(Monochamus scutellatus)

up to 1.25 inches long; elongated oval gray to dark gray body; two small white spots at base of wing coverings; long legs and very long curving antennae; larvae are wood borers on evergreen trees

Golden Tortoise Beetle ⓥ
(Charidotella sexpunctata)

up to 0.28 inch long; round body; shiny golden to tawny red with black spots; wing coverings and pronotum extended to cover legs and head; adults and larvae are plant feeders

European Crane Fly (P)
(Tipula paludosa)

up to 1.1 inches long; long narrow brown body, very long legs and transparent wings; resembles a giant mosquito; larvae feed on grass roots

Mosquito Larva (P)
(Family Culicidae)

up to 0.2 inch long; aquatic living near surface; elongated brown segmented body with no legs and a long breathing siphon on the rear end; often wiggles back and forth in the water

Long-legged Fly (V) (B)
(Family Dolichopodidae)

up to 0.35 inch; highly variable color body; bright eyes; mostly transparent wings and long, thin legs; often seen perching on leaves; adults prey on other insects, including aphids, spider mites, thrips, and whiteflies

Greater Bee Fly ⊛ (V)
(Bombylius major)

up to 0.5 inch long; bulbous body with generally golden-brown hair; two clear wings edged with black, and a rigid, forward-pointing proboscis; resembles a small bumblebee; adults hover and feed at flowers; larvae are parasites of bee and wasp nests

House Fly (P)
(Musca domestica)

up to 0.3 inch long; gray hairy body with black stripes on the thorax, two transparent wings, and red eyes; attracted to garbage, animal waste, and decaying material

Greenbottle Fly
(Genus *Lucilia*)

up to 0.4 inch long; hairy, metallic green to coppery body; two transparent wings; reddish eyes; feeds on flower nectar, pollen; attracted to animal waste, carrion, and decaying material

Flesh Fly
(Family Sarcophagidae)

up to 0.4 inch long; hairy gray body with black stripes; two transparent wings; red eyes; feeds on flower nectar; attracted to animal waste, decaying material, animal wounds

Black-margined Flower Fly
(*Syrphus opinator*)

up to 0.45 inch long; large eyes; dark thorax with short golden hairs; two transparent wings generally held angled away from the body; black abdomen with yellow bands; bee mimic

Margined Calligrapher
(*Toxomerus marginatus*)

up to 0.25 inch long; large eyes; two clear wings held out to the side; orange-and-black abdomen that tapers to the rear; larvae feed on aphids and other soft bodied ineect pests

Early Tachinid Fly
(*Epalpus signifer*)

to 0.4 inch long; robust body; large eyes; brown thorax with thin black stripes; bulbout spiny black abdomen with pale patch near the tip; two clear wings; parasitoid of other insects, particulary caterpillars

Narcissus Bulb Fly
(*Merodon equestris*)

to 0.55 inch long; stout hairy black-and-golden body; large eyes; two transparent wings; mimics a bee; larvae feed on plant bulbs in the amaryllis family

Robber Fly Ⓥ Ⓑ
(Family Asilidae)

up to 1 inch long; highly variable in appearance; typically slender body with a tapered abdomen; large eyes; two wings; and long, bristly legs; opportunistic predators of other insects; perches on vegetation or structures and flies out to capture prey; some are bee mimics

European Earwig Ⓟ Ⓑ
(Forficula auricularia)

up to 0.55 inch long; elongated dark brown body; wingless; prominent pinchers on the end of the abdomen; male pinchers strait, female pinchers curved; omnivorous, occasionally nibbles on plants; beneficial predator of other insects

Brown Marmorated Stink Bug **P**
(Halyomorpha halys)

up to 0.7 inch long; brown shield-shaped body with long, banded antennae, and light and dark bands on the edge of the abdomen; wingless nymphs are gray-brown marked with red; vegetable and fruit pest; nuisance pest entering homes; invasive

Small Milkweed Bug **V** **P**
(Lygaeus kalmii)

up to 0.5 inch; elongated oval red-and-dark gray body with black wing tips marked with light spots; wingless nymphs orange and black; feeds on plant sap from leaves and on stems and seeds of milkweed; adults may also consume aphids and monarch eggs and young larvae

North American Tarnished Plant Bug **P** **D**
(Lygus lineolaris)

up to 0.25 inch long; oval body marked with yellow, brown, and black; long antennae; feeds by piercing plant tissues; attacks a wide range of plants; transmits plant diseases

Bordered Plant Bug **P**
(Largus spp.)

up to 0.5 inch; adult with oval dark gray-blue-to-black body with orange around the edges; wingless nymphs are shiny black with a central red spot; feeds on ornamental plants and berries; generally causes little damage, but can scar fruit

Rhododendron Leafhopper **P**
(Graphocephala fennahi)

up to 0.35 inch long; elongated bright-green body; forewings with reddish stripes

Giant Water Bug **V**
(Lethocerus americanus)

up to 2.25 inches long; brown, oval body; large front legs; aquatic; attracted to artificial lights at night; can inflict painful bite

Spined Soldier Bug **B**
(Podisus maculiventris)

up to 0.6 inch long; mottled brown shield-shaped body with one spine on each shoulder and a dark diamond on back where the wings overlap; predatory, feeding on insects, including many common pests

Green Stink Bug **P**
(Chinavia hilaris)

up to 0.75 inch long; green shield-shaped body with slightly darker diamond shape on the back where wings overlap; nymphs wingless and marked with black, orange, yellow, and white; feeds on plant juices; pest of many vegetable, fruit, and landscape plants

Masked Hunter **B**
(Reduvius personatus)

up to 0.85 inch long; elliptical, somewhat flattened, black body; wings folded over back; noticeable curved beak under head

Jagged Ambush Bug **B**
(Phymata americana)

up to 0.35 inch long; jagged somewhat hourglass-shaped yellow body mottled with brown; membranous wings; enlarged front legs for grasping prey; a sit-and-wait predator found on flowers, particularly goldenrod

Consperse Stink Bug **P**
(Euchistus conspersus)

up to 0.5 inch long; brown shield-shaped body with slightly darker diamond shape on the back where wings overlap; nymphs wingless; plant pest

Green Peach Aphid Ⓟ Ⓓ
(Myzus persicae)

up to 0.08 inch; yellow-green pear-shaped body with dark eyes; adults may be winged or not; pest of many vegetables and fruit trees; transmit plant diseases

Cottony Maple Scale Ⓟ
(Pulvinaria innumerabilis)

up to 0.15 inch long; brown, flattened body; individuals secrete noticeable white cottony wax, making it look much larger

Greenhouse Whitefly Ⓟ Ⓓ
(Trialeurodes vaporariorum)

up to 0.08 inch long; yellow body and four white, powdery wings; feeds on plant sap; indoor and greenhouse plant pest; outdoor garden pest during the summer

Western Boxelder Bug Ⓟ
(Boisea rubrolineata)

up to 0.5 inch long; elliptical black body marked with red lines; abdomen red; adults have wings; nymphs are wingless

Oleander Aphid Ⓟ Ⓓ
(Aphis nerii)

up to 0.1 inch long; bulbous yellow body with black legs, antennae, and eyes; has two black pipe-like projections on the abdomen; adults may or may not have wings; nymphs look like small adults; feeds on plant sap and is a pest of Oleander *(Nerium oleander)* and milkweeds *(Asclepias* spp.); honeydew also causes sooty mold on plants

Western Flower Thrips **P** **D**
(Frankliniella occidentalis)

up to 0.08 inch; tiny elongated yellow-green bodies with pale, feathery wings; feeds on plant juices; causes plant discoloration or deformation; attacks many plants, including vegetables, fruit trees, berries, flowers,l and ornamentals

Green Lacewing **V**
(Chrysoperla spp.)

up to 0.7 inch long; light green slender body, long antennae, golden eyes, and four transparent wings with green veins; adults feed on pollen and nectar; often attracted to artificial lights at night

Green Lacewing Larva **B**
(Chrysoperla spp.)

up to 0.5 inch long; elongated mottled brown body tapered toward the rear; large jaws; resembles a small alligator; ferocious predator of soft-bodied pests, including aphids, whiteflies, spider mites, and thrips

Western Honey Bee  **V**
(Apis mellifera)

up to 0.75 inch long; fuzzy appearance, black eyes, four amber wings; black-and golden-orange-striped abdomen; carries pollen on back legs; produces large colonies; can aggressively defend hives; exceptional pollinator

Golden Paper Wasp **B**
(Polistes aurifer)

up to 0.5 inch long; dark thorax; elongated golden abdomen marked with black; four narrow amber wings; and a distinct waist between the abdomen and thorax; social; often constructs nest on structures or in cavities; adults are predatory on other insects, including pest species; can sting

European Paper Wasp **P** **B**
(Polistes dominula)

up to 0.5 inch long; elongated black body marked with yellow; four narrow amber wings; a distinct waist between the abdomen and thorax; social; invasive; often constructs nest on structures; adults are predatory on other insects, including pest species; can sting

Western Paper Wasp **P** **B**
(Mischocyttarus flavitarsis)

up to 0.65 inch long; elongated black body marked with yellow; abdomen golden striped with black; long legs, dark amber wings; social

Western Yellow Jacket **P** **B**
(Vespula pensylvanica)

up to 0.7 inch long; elongated black-and-yellow body; four amber wings; yellow-striped abdomen; colonial; constructs papery nests, often in cavities in the ground; adults are predatory on other insects, including pest species; aggressively defends nests and stings; seeks out sugary foods and can be a nuisance

Bald-faced Hornet 🐝 🅿 🅱
(Dolichovespula maculata)

up to 0.75 inch long; black with white to cream markings and clear amber wings; social; creates spherical papery nest typically in vegetation; can deliver painful sting

Odorous House Ants 🅿
(Tapinoma sessile)

up to 0.12 inch long; tiny, dark brown to black body; can form large colonies; seeks out sugary foods, considered a nuisance pest

Red Pavement Ant 🅿
(Tetramorium caespitum)

up to 0.12 inches long; tiny; dark reddish-brown-to-almost black body; form large colonies, often around homes and other structures

Western Thatching Ant 🐝 🅱
(Formica obscuripes)

up to 0.4 inch long, but workers are smaller; dull black body, rounded abdomen with darker stripes; narrow, reddish head; constructs large, dome-shaped mounded nests composed of debris found in the nearby area; predatory on other arthropods

Yellow-legged Mud Dauber Wasp 🐝 🅿
(Sceliphron caementarium)

up to 1 inch long; black body marked with yellow; long, thin legs; four narrow, dark wings; abdomen with a long, narrow waist; preys on spiders; builds nests out of mud, often on structures

Common Blue Mud Dauber Wasp 🐝 🅿 🅱
(Chalybion californicum)

up to 0.9 inch long; elongated metallic blue body and wings; long legs, narrow waist; often creates mud nests on buildings or structures

Bicolored Striped Sweat Bee 🐝 Ⓥ
(Agapostemon virescens)

up to 0.45 inch long; metallic green head and thorax; black abdomen striped with yellow; amber wings

Texas Striped Sweat Bee 🐝 Ⓥ
(Agapostemon texanus)

up to 0.5 inch long; head and thorax metallic green, dark, narrow wings; abdomen metallic green in females or yellow with black bands in males; avid flower visitor

Blue Orchard Bee 🐝 Ⓥ
(Osmia lignaria)

up to 0.55 inch long; compact black body with bluish iridescence; clear wings; nests in natural holes in wood; also use bee boxes

Yellow-faced Bumble Bee 🐝 Ⓥ
(Bombus vosnesenskii)

up to 0.8 inch long; stout, fuzzy black body; head and front part of thorax yellow; abdomen tip yellow

Hunt's Bumble Bee 🐝 Ⓥ
(Bombus huntii)

up to 0.6 inch long; fuzzy, robust body with a black-and-yellow pattern; abdomen with reddish band in center; four black wings; carries pollen on hind legs; colonial; nests in underground cavities

Great Basin Bumble Bee 🐝 Ⓥ
(Bombus centralis)

up to 0.6 inch long; stout yellow-and-black fuzzy body; abdomen yellow with two wide reddish-orange bands separated by black

European Mantis Ⓥ Ⓑ
(Mantis religiosa)

up to 3 inches long; slender green-to-brown body; triangular head; enlarged front legs for grasping prey; immatures lack wings; adults have four wings

GRASSHOPPERS, CRICKETS, & KATYDIDS
Order Orthoptera

Jerusalem Cricket Ⓥ Ⓟ
(Stenopelmatus spp.)

up to 2.5 inches long; tawny brown head, tan legs, large hind legs; long antennae and a bulbous black-striped pale abdomen; flightless; subterranian and nocturnal; often coming to lights at night; feeds on other insects and plant roots; often attacking potatoes, carrots, and other vegetables

Field Cricket Ⓥ Ⓑ
(Gryllus spp.)

up to 1.2 inches long; dark brown to black with membranous wings, enlarged hind legs, long antennae, and two prominent tail filaments; omnivores; produce loud chirping calls

Carolina Grasshopper Ⓥ
(Dissosteira carolina)

up to 2.25 inches long; long narrow gray-to-brown mottled body; long powerful hind legs for jumping; four mebranous wings; hindwings black with broad pale border visible during flight; often rests on open ground

Two–striped Grasshopper
(Melanoplus bivittatus)

up to 2.1 inches long; long narrow
brown-and-tan or brown-and-yellow
body; long powerful hind legs for
jumping; four mebranous wings

Migratory Grasshopper
(Melanoplus sanguinipes)

up to 1.1 inches long; long narrow
mottled yellow-and-brown body;
long powerful hind legs for jumping;
four mebranous wings; hind legs with
dark bands

Western Tree Cricket
(Oecanthus californicus)

up to 0.7 inch long; narrow green, yel-
lowish to light brown body tapered at
both ends; rounded clear wings; make
long, continuous trill call

Mormon Cricket
(Anabrus simplex)

up to 1.75 inches long; color variable
from green, black, or brown; robust
body; long antennae and hind legs;
females with long ovipositor off the
back of the abdomen

Fork-tailed Bush Katydid
(Scudderia furcata)

up to 1.8 inches long; robust bright
green body; long antennae; long hind
legs and green membranous wings;
looks like a leaf; feeds on plants

COCKROACHES & TERMITES
Order Blattodea

American Cockroach V P
(Periplaneta americana)

up to 2 inches long; oblong, reddish-brown body, spiny legs, and long antennae; adults have brown membranous wings; common under objects or mulch; scavenger; nocturnal

DRAGONFLIES & DAMSELFLIES
Order Odonata

Common Green Darner V B
(Anax junius)

up to 3.1 inches long; large eyes; green thorax; long blue-to-brown abdomen; four transparent wings

Common Whitetail V B
(Plathemis lydia)

up to 2 inches long; elongated body; male with dark head, chalky white abdomen, and four clear wings with a central black band; females with brown abdomen spoted with white

Four-spotted Skimmer V B
(Libellula quadrimaculata)

up to 1.7 inches long; brown body with long, slender abdomen marked with black at the tip; four transparent wings marked with four small black spots

Twelve-spotted Skimmer V B
(Libellula pulchella)

up to 2 inches long; large eyes; male with powdery white body and transparent wings marked with 12 dark spots and 8 white spots; female body brown and wings marked with 12 dark spots

Western Pondhawk V B
(Erythemis collocata)

up to 1.6 inches long; large eyes; male with powdery blue body; female with green body marked with brown; with four transparent wings

Sowbug and Pillbug **B**
(Order Isopoda)

up to 0.45 inch long; dark gray-to-brown, oval body, with plate-like segments and seven pairs of small legs; feeds on decaying plant material; found under objects, leaf litter, and mulch

Two-spotted Spider Mite **P**
(Tetranychus urticae)

up to 0.03 inch long; oval yellow-to-orange body; four pairs of legs; often two visible dark side spots; resembles a tiny spider; feeds on plant sap and spins loose silk on vegetation; pest of many trees and shrubs, vegetables, and berries

European Harvestmen **B**
(Phalangium opilio)

brown body up to 0.3 inch long with eight much longer, thin legs; predatory

Milky Slug **P** **B**
(Deroceras reticulatum)

up to 2.3 inches long; elongated mottled gray-to-brown slimy body with a hump on the back; two stalk-like tentacles off the head; pest of vegetables, flowers, and some fruits

Yellow Garden Spider **V** **B**
(Argiope aurantia)

up to 2.5 inches long; abdomen egg-shaped with black-and-yellow markings; eight black legs marked with yellow or red; females much larger than males; spins large, circular web with distinctive central zigzag pattern to capture prey

Stone Centipede **P** **B**
(Order Lithobiomorpha)

up to 1.1 inches long; elongated flat reddish-brown body; long antennae and many legs out to the side; typically found under logs, rock or leaf litter; predaceous

Zebra Jumping Spider **V** **B**
(*Salticus scenicus*)

to 0.35 inch long; black body and eight legs; abdomen blackish brown striped with white; legs marked with white; prominent forward-facing eyes; active predators; often seen on plants, buildings, and other structures

Banded Garden Spider **V** **B**
(*Argiope trifasciata*)

body up to 2.5 inches long, abdomen egg-shaped with black and yellow bands; eight black legs marked with orange; females much larger than males; spins large circular web to capture prey

Cross Orbweaver **V** **B**
(*Araneus diadematus*)

females up to 0.75 inch, male much smaller; eight legs; bulbous orange-brown to grayish abdomen marked with white spots and a white cross; makes large web for capturing prey

Goldenrod Crab Spider **V** **B**
(*Misumena vatia*)

up to 0.4 inch long; crab-like body with eight legs and bulbous abdomen; abdomen may have some reddish markings; sit-and-wait predator on flowers; body color changes with flower color

House Centipede  **B**
(Scutigera coleoptrata)

up to 1.3 inches long; long slender brown body marked with black stripes; long antennae; many pairs of long delicate legs out to the side; predatory; often found in buildings

Western Fire Centipede **B**
(Scolopocryptops gracilis)

up to 1.7 inches long; long reddish-brown body; two antennae and many paler legs out to the side; predatory; can bite

Garden Snail **B**
(Cornu aspersum)

highly variable size, 0.2 to 4 inches; brown to dull-colored fleshy body with elongated stalk-like tentacles off the head; a hard shell on the back; feeds on organic material